Atria

Atria

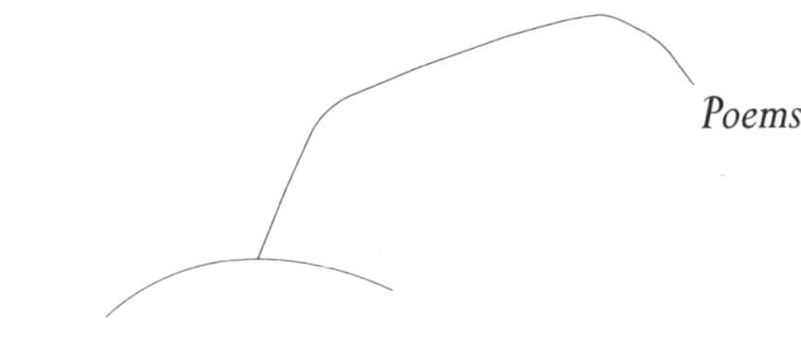

Poems

D.S. WALDMAN

Liveright Publishing Corporation

A Division of W. W. Norton & Company
Independent Publishers Since 1923

Printed in the United States of America
First Edition

For information about special discounts for bulk purchases, please contact W. W. Norton Special Sales at specialsales@wwnorton.com or 800-233-4830

Manufacturing by Versa Press
Book design by Anna Knighton
Production manager: Gwen Cullen

ISBN 978-1-324-09726-6

Liveright Publishing Corporation, 500 Fifth Avenue, New York, NY 10110
www.wwnorton.com

W. W. Norton & Company Ltd., 15 Carlisle Street, London W1D 3BS

Authorized EU representative: EAS, Mustamäe tee 50, 10621 Tallinn, Estonia

1 2 3 4 5 6 7 8 9 0

Contents

Atria

The relation between what we see
and what we know is never settled.

—JOHN BERGER

Calder

It is the act of entering that creates loneliness. I stand, at first, in the corner and can't bear it, the stillness of them—a child looking up from a crib, reaching. The door at my back leads to a balcony and is locked, boxing wind out of the composition.

The thing about art and especially three-dimensional art is I expect it, always, to teach me something. The dialogue between the sun and dew flowers tracking east. The head turning to catch in its gaze the leg of a stranger as they leave the room. I begin to move, to walk about the mobiles.

Outside, on the balcony, leaves skitter in wind. Daylight in and out behind clouds. *In the dream I've been having lately*, is how one might begin a poem in this room. In mine, at a party, I look up and am told I'm the oldest in the room by *several rotations*. A condemnation. A measure of both time and distance.

Last night, waking from this or another dream, I looked through a scatter of Polaroids on the bedside table. In one, she stands next to a Joshua tree. The sky is blue and cold and she smiles, mouth closed, at the camera.

A family enters and the child moves about the mobiles in a whorl, a step ahead of his mother. Sunlight in a wedge on the wall, over a quotation from the artist: *Disparity in form, color, size, weight, motion is what makes a composition*. And when the child reaches for one of them, one of the red spades accenting the dark wire, his mother waits. She lets him touch it, once and briefly, before taking away his hand.

Tisch

(1962) Oil on canvas

For once in California the rain is total.
The bay a different shade of sky, Payne's Gray.

On the train to the museum, at the Embarcadero stop
with my father, I start to get emotional. Tender as ever, having
told a woman who loves me I cannot, or
can no longer, love her.

I want him to see but he doesn't. I ask instead if there's
anything in particular he'd like to see at MOMA.
Photography or sculpture. Abstract painting.

I walk until I find a room to be alone in, a room full
of Richter. Nostalgia, says the wall. Erasure. History.
A sense of displacement. I take a picture of the plaque.

The paintings in this room are based on photographs.
Behind me, a rendering of his wife, the artist Sabine Moritz
reading a magazine. In front of me, the cloud—
the vast smudge obscuring the white table—is not paint,
as I'd assumed, but turpentine. It says on the wall.

Rain just audible from the gallery bridge. It's slow,
slowing, but refuses an altogether break.

My father, later, will tell me of a piece on another floor
called *Vortex*, a warped and convex sheet
of lacquered fiberglass. It's a mirror, he will say,
but you can't see yourself.

The intimacy of a crowded museum is not unlike the intimacy
of an empty room. Having feelings. Watching them pass.

I stay here until my father texts that he's seen what
he's needed to see. Through occasional gaps, seams in the crowd,
I can see him standing by the stairs. He asks
where he can meet me. If I'm hungry.
Do I know how to get home from here.

The Köln Concert

We showed up with a U-Haul and a Prius and could not see the ocean. "They lay it on thick there," a friend had said of Pacifica, "two, three weeks at a time." We pulled off at the bluffs before taking our things to the cottage on Winona. Five hours it took for the cat to fall asleep, and the door chimes woke him. The Pacific was hard and restless in the fog.

It was entirely improvised, they say. An hour and six minutes streaming back and forth between jazz and classical, and broken across four parts. The concert became famous, in part, because of the quality of the audience, careful as they were not to applaud or cry out until Jarrett had entirely stopped playing. You can hear in the recording, at the end of each section, a moment of full silence before the crowd erupts.

I heard it for the first time that summer, on recommendation from a dying poet. I listened on gray walks to the seawall, the weed store, a coffee shop with no bathroom or food service. It was June and I was half-zipped in a winter coat. Our cottage was small, 800 square feet, so we took calls with our therapists in the Prius. I walked by on my way in from the cliffs, pretending I hadn't noticed her. The cat swished his tail at the screen door.

Critics dubbed his a "homesick lyricism," celebrating Jarrett's merging of the modern and the nostalgic. His long, uninterrupted improvisations were punctuated, almost always, with moments of dissonance, his hands playing at two different time signatures. "A sort of churning," the late poet had said, "like he's clearing the chalkboard between movements." I found myself listening for these slippages, harmony giving way, one hand dancing into a different time.

Bly wrote a poem titled "Listening to the Köln Concert," which I read years before knowing the concert or Keith Jarrett. "The notes abandon so much as they move," he writes; and later in the stanza, "the music is my attention to you."

A creek ran downhill past the cottage and emptied somewhere into Blue Whale Cove. We knew no one, just our landlord and his adult son, and we'd walk along the wrinkled creekwater. The path took us to that same lookout, our point of origin. It was rare to see more than twenty yards out into the cove, but a handful of times in August the fog burned off, the sky shock blue. The first whale we saw was young and curious, breaching on one, then the other side of a small fishing boat. L saw it first and got very quiet. Then she took me by the hand, and said my name.

At Lake Merritt

Together we inventoried the body's urgencies. Make a list, she said, try less to think than to feel. My left earbud had run out of battery, so here and there I was distracted by the clatter of skateboarders kickflipping in the parking lot, or trying to. It sort of had me off kilter. Thoughts are of the body too, I thought or said, knowing's a filter for sensation. A ways off in the middle of the lake a rower broke the surface in long strokes. Anxiety in the chest, blooming. One or two points of tension in the low back. A bit of light through clouds, slow to reach me. Marissa wasn't the first therapist to suggest I make a list. Excuse me, said the person who'd appeared in my periphery, excuse me. But I pointed to my earbud that did not work, mouthed sorry. He made this little gesture with his thumb, miming a lighter—I don't know how it is for you, but I wish to have everything for anyone who asks, and briefly I thought to share this with Marissa, a mid-behavior adjustment. But I knew she'd have us pivot to Matty again, that I'd have to bring up the anniversary. Sorry, I mouthed once more, and shook my head. Pinpricks of sweat at the hairline. Numbness gradual through the toes. I got up from the bench and checked the time on my phone—I could hear Marissa stifle a cough. My mother had texted. The date a headline for her words, Thinking of you XO. A sort of closing of the throat. I'd been in Maine when it happened, this rural coastline with no cell service, so I didn't get his voice note until after he'd gone into a coma. Hey it's been a while, just checking in on you, seeing how the weather is up in Small Point. Holler sometime. I still have it saved on my phone, a sealed vial of his smoker's timbre. Save everything. Buy the terabyte and save everything, every text and photo and voicemail. Only once the sun had slipped again behind clouds, once the rower was gone past a bend in the shoreline and a group of runners parted around me, did I realize Marissa was speaking again. Looking at the list, she said, looking at what's happening in your body tell me what feels least tolerable. Or maybe she said, Tell me what you can live with and what you can no longer carry. Language is everything in therapy. I swiped back to the list. I wanted a cigarette. The man from before sat on a concrete slab among the skateboarders in the round empty lot. I watched the skateboarder he was watching, a tall kid with no shirt, long jean shorts down to the tops of his socks. It wasn't a kickflip he was trying but a long jump down the stairs to the bike path where I stood by the water. He gestured for me to step aside a little, and I did, and I waved. Dull ache in the hips. Simple excitement at being addressed. Try it, said Marissa, try telling me that.

HOWL, eon (I, II)

My mother cranes to take in the mural—dusk blue
and livid in what light it gathers. Underlayers of text
no longer legible. Then what I can only call marks,
the way Basquiat did it
except that these do not figure or represent.
She is transfixed by a neat white square, alone
in the bottom-left corner, the only real geometry.

This is the Polaroid I take of her, from behind, the white
of her hair in conversation with a patch of glare—
the paint is incandescent. *Preservation*, says the artist statement,
and its counterpart, *annihilation*. My mother takes the camera
from my hands while I put on my corduroy—
        she was a photographer,
old-process mostly, platinum palladium
and cyanotypes, chemical baths in the living room.
We will go, later, across town
to meet L at a place called Wild Seed.

A video on loop in the atrium shows Mehretu
in-process. Industrial rollers spreading ink and paint
in wide swaths across the canvas, a strange perforated tool
        for texture.
The artist sits on a bench looking up
at the unfinished mural. She wears headphones, holds
a can of black spray paint.

Tonight we will eat mushroom fritters, some sort of crudo.

We will drink activated charcoal and toast to health,
good company, the future.
I will lay the photo among knives
and napkins and tell L how Mehretu
began with a foundation of digital images, distorted photographs
of street protests, landscapes of the American west.
I will say how hard it is to get a good picture
of my mother, and my mother will take the last photo
of L and me. Black and white, the hand
of our server visible in the bottom-right, removing my plate.

My mother hands me the Polaroid by its strap.
She frees the collar of my jacket, pulls it snug
around my neck. It is not winter in the city
but it is cold, and I tell her to wait
in the atrium while I bring the car around.

The Clarinet

(1913) 37½ × 47⅜ papier collé

I wake in midwinter with a stranger

A study of pictorial constitution
I know from a book on my desk. The collage

Is in an hour, and we haven't brushed

Or established boundaries for the medium
I tell her the instrument vanishes

from Chino, her shoes on the floor

its subject the faintest thing in the frame
And Gabby explains how she got the scar

The cat tangled in our shoes by the vent

It's just still-life, with varied perspective
or blacktop haze. I tell her the story

Within the oval frame—a sign appears

Resumes but off-kilter, as through water
Don't use that in a poem, she tells me

The boyfriend in France, my ex down the road

A little sand, here and there, in the pigment
That newer edgy dating app—it was

The illusory appearance of depth

Like a floorboard offers texture, or how
Ok you can use it, but don't mention

The scar I hide with longer sleeves. I mean

That tactile qualities define a space
A ride to the station, though I could walk

Is music. A suggestion of music

Point Reyes

Drove to where the trees turn to ocean air and vista,
golden hills and old crag, water churning
in the far, low distances. M brought enough to microdose
and we chewed dried persimmon to help
with the aftertaste: sort of chemical but earthy.
And the elk we'd come to see watched us
in a herd, interested then not, pulling grass and chewing.
We knew to be nonthreatening. There were three of us
then four, but J passed on the mushrooms. Our keeper,
he walked between us and the rocky ledges.
"This ocean," wrote Spicer, "humiliating in its disguises."
We took turns talking horizon-like about love,
making up a future we could remember
or want to, careful always when we saw a calf nearby
with its mother: they'll charge you.
As far north and south as we could see, at a pace
we could not, cliffs spilled into the Pacific
whose shimmer belonged to none of us
and each of us, in turns. "Tougher than anything."
And the long moments opened around us
and the bag of persimmon rounds grew light.
Cold-air breath a familiar hurt. A stirring white from blue,
the patterned sounding. We'd all return, eventually
and alone, to our expensive rooms in the city, the ebbing
traffic of late evening on MacArthur. We'd never make it
to the far point at trail's end, the point for which the park
is named, and where no elk were grazing.

Man Ray

Every piece in its frame, behind glass, is really two works. There's the rayograph, its vaporous, everyday shapes drifting across the once light-sensitive paper. And over it, caught in the glass, a spontaneous portrait of the viewer, startled to confront himself.

• • •

After the conversation, after she threw her things into bags, I stood a while in what remained. A bed, two rugs, a place to sit. On the fridge, every photo of us together. Polaroids from Joshua Tree. Ocean Beach. Golden Gate Park.

• • •

As ever, I write down my reactions to things. I attempt to tie Cubism to camera-less photography. Filling one side of the paper with scrawl, I flip it over and find, in semi-cursive, the note she wrote the night before leaving. It begins, *This is what I know:*

• • •

In the previous gallery, I stood a while in front of an early Braque, the everyday objects present in an otherwise splintered composition. I do that here, with the rayograph. *Three fingers of the right hand / A key on a string / Cheese grater?* When I run out of space to write, I bring out my phone.

• • •

The picture—my photo of a photo framed in glass—is complicated by glare and reflection, the ideal beauty of the key obscured. I move right, attempt to block the light with my body, removing myself from the composition.

The Lake

After dinner with Gabby a few weeks back at my mom's—scatter of photos on the fridge—I recounted some of our favorite places on the farm and around town. The big lake with no dock where Matty and I fished for carp in the summer. Rupp Arena for the Louisville game around New Year's. Some friend's dad's lot on the north side where we shot cans off the hood of a rusted-over hatchback. Could have killed each other, I told Gabby, bad as we were with a rifle. Looking at her looking at the photos, I thought back to that text he sent a few months before he died. I'd been going through a rough stretch and crushed seven or eight Klonopins in a glass of orange juice and shut myself in the car, passed out before I could turn the key. You can't have a phone in those hospitals, so I didn't see it until I got discharged. Dan I love you. Can't overdose on those. See you in a few days. It'd take like eighty to kill you, apparently. We met up at the lake the day I got out—we hadn't been there together in ages—and I told him about some of the people I met, how this woman named Barbara kept calling me a prospect. I realized, as I was telling the story to Gabby, that it was the last time I saw him, there in the tall grass in his undershirt, the car door slung open, Neil Young on the radio. Overhead the Kentucky sky was clear and went on forever. I don't really remember how we parted or where I went after, only that he wanted to stay a while, that at some point he hugged me, tucked a cig behind his ear, and started down toward the water.

Low Poetics: A Meditation

Twenty years ago I was in an accident that resulted in the loss of function and feeling in my right hand. I was a child playing ice hockey. A friend's skate found, somehow, the underside of my wrist. There was a lot of blood. There was surgery. Years of physical therapy. I'd been, at the time, right-handed.

Being young—I was eleven when the accident occurred—there was a chance I could regain some degree of sensation and movement, and over time I did. But from the moment I woke in the hospital it was clear I could no longer claim right-handedness; the surgeon was quick to tell me so. I could no longer move through the world relying—consciously or not—on the dexterity and coordination of the hand I'd entered the world (if that's how it works) using.

The process of switching to my left was not swift, and in fact I would say it's ongoing. Writing. Brushing my teeth. Using silverware. Throwing darts. What were once tasks performed without thought became, and to some degree remain, little problems to be solved. There was once more or less a single way I picked up a pen, gripped it, wrote my name; and overnight I had to develop a new way, had to experiment with the foreign clumsiness of my left, puzzle toward what felt most right or comfortable. And as I read back over this paragraph, the process sounds very much like an experience of limitation—for years I would have described it this way, having something, and having it taken away.

•

On the second floor of SFMOMA, on the first wall one sees upon entering the permanent galleries, there hangs a brown-scale painting whose composition gives the impression of splintered wood. It has always looked, to me, like the artist shattered a cello across a hardwood floor and, with the resulting shards, created a semi-sculptural object which they then painted. The artist is cubist innovator Georges Braque, the painting, *Still Life (Violin and Candlestick)* (1910).

In so far as there were objectives attached to the development of cubism—to early cubist works by Braque and his collaborator-from-afar, Pablo Picasso—they had to do with presenting, within a single composition, subjects and forms from a number of vantage points. The titular candlestick in Braque's painting, for example, is identifiable in profile in the painting's center. That is, we experience it from the side, as we might upon entering a room, seeing it on a dining room table. Directly behind this representation of the candlestick, though, we also see its base, tilted upward, as though we were looking directly down onto the object. This perspective-play allows the viewer multiple ways of seeing, experiencing, contemplating the candlestick, and also opens a formal conversation between the upward tilted base—which is round—and the painting's other primary object, the violin, whose rounded body is recognizable, if fragmented, in the bottom left corner of the composition.

In the relationship between the candlestick and the violin—or at least in the shards of them available to the viewer—I experience something of a lyric association. Despite the compositional distance between the two forms—that they are not placed side-by-side—they announce themselves, though subtly, as linked through their shared roundness within a composition I might otherwise characterize as geometrical and splintered. "The subject is not the object," wrote Braque, "it is the new unity, the lyricism which stems entirely from the means employed." He's speaking here, partly, in the language of poetry. And I take this quotation to mean that the objects in the painting, the candlestick and violin—what, in poetry, we might refer to as *content*—are in cubism less important than how, compositionally, these objects relate to one another—*form*. There's something profound to me in how, from different and distinct places in a fractured and hard-edged composition, these rounded shapes seem to find each other.

•

Cultural critic Jack Halberstam, in their book *The Queer Art of Failure*, uses the term "low theory" to describe a mode of thinking that refutes binaries and "tries to locate all the in-between spaces," a knowledge practice that "revels in the detours, twists, and turns through knowing and confusion, and that seeks not to explain but to involve." I am no longer right-handed, but would also not say I am left-handed. I wrote this essay by hand, for example, with my left, but if called upon to draw a circle on a canvas or chalkboard I would probably use my right. I inhabit an in-between space, a region between the singular demand of a task—write your name here—and the myriad ways I might accomplish the task.

In Braque's painting, I'm quick to associate the rounded, upturned candlestick base with the rounded outer edge of the violin. That doesn't mean I'm right or that it was the artist's intention for all viewers to see a connection between these forms; it's simply where my mind goes, my gaze. Search the internet for an image of this painting—where is *your* gaze drawn?

•

Looking at *Violin and Candlestick*, I'm reminded of John Ashbery's early love poem "Some Trees," in particular its opening lines: "These are amazing: each / Joining a neighbor, as though speech / Were a still performance." I'm reminded, especially, of how in just a few lines the trees from the poem's title become something spoken, or a replacement for language—how, through a quick series of sonic linkages, the word "trees" becomes, or at least develops a lyric connection to, the word "speech." *Trees—These—each—speech*—we hear the word evolve down the page, and though there exists a logical gap between where we began (trees) and where we find ourselves (speech), there is a certain subconscious trust one has in rhyme and assonance which allows, in the reader's mind, for an associative relationship to open between two seemingly disparate words. Suddenly, the entangled trees are an expression of love, or perhaps are what, of love, language fails to capture. *It is the new unity, the lyricism which stems entirely from the means employed.*

•

My experience of Braque's work, and of this painting in particular, is not wholly passive. I'm finding that part of why I return so often to *Violin and Candlestick*—as opposed to other paintings in the same gallery; say, O'Keeffe's *Lake George*—is that the act of viewing feels very much like a generative act. I'm invited into the composition, encouraged to identify, across the greater painting, shapes and shards and forms that seem to want to be seen together, puzzled together and reconstituted on a canvas only I can see. I'm allowed, that is, my own unique experience of the art. And it's for similar reasons that, as a reader, I'm drawn often to poems one might describe as especially elliptical or fragmented.

The title sequence in *Mean Free Path*—the third poetry collection of Ben Lerner, an aesthetic descendant of Ashbery's—spans thirty-four pages over two sections of the book and is at its core, like "Some Trees," a love poem. Or it is at least a poem that, in content and procedure, engages with—maybe challenges the possibility of—the love poem as a mode:

> To keep light from the object falling
> Gently on a little clearing. They call this
> Like rain that never reaches ground
> Reading, like birds that lure predators away
> Virga, or the failure of the gaze to reach

Sentences in this poem do not begin, necessarily, where the line begins, and almost never continue from one line to another. They peter out, stop short; they sometimes resume later in the poem, and sometimes never return.

"Rain that never reaches ground," for example, refers to the meteorological phenomenon virga, which in the poem appears not in the line after its description, but two lines down. Syntactically, the meteorological description is applied to the word "reading"—as if to say, no single reading can "reach ground," can bridge the gap between the poet's creation and the reader's interpretation.

I personally hear, in Lerner's poem, a speaker trying over and over to formulate language in proportion to their feelings—and over and over, failing, having to recapitulate, try again.

And that's love // And that's elegy

The reader is left, then, not with a poem that proceeds linearly, but rather a poem that offers many ways to proceed, conditions ripe with possibility, interpretational plurality. "The aim," according to Braque, "is not to reconstitute an anecdotal fact, but to constitute a pictorial fact." I feel the invitation to enter *Mean Free Path*, to make my own associations and meanings, leaps between ideas and images positioned not necessarily next to each other, compositionally. The gaze, in this type of work, cannot fail to reach. It lands where it lands.

•

I can't say with certainty that the disability I live with, and the daily puzzling it requires, has necessarily prepared me in some way to experience the art of Braque, Ashbery, or Lerner. But I know for sure that when the teller at the bodega on the corner of Perkins and Grand hands me my change, I have to pause a moment—I have to decide which hand to extend to receive the money, whether I can afford the gesture without losing grip of the groceries I'm holding. I know for sure that these moments, my days, are little puzzles.

I feel welcomed by, welcomed into, such paintings as *Violin and Candlestick*, such poems as "Mean Free Path." This type of art offers experiences not of singular, linear interpretation, but of multitude—the question becomes not *Do you see it?* or, in the poems, *Do you get it?* but rather, *What do you see? What is your reading?*

Today at the store I needed eggs and fruit, crackers, two large bottles of sparkling water, and a block of cheese. The man at the register extended two singles, a few coins. My hands were full and he put the change on the counter. I told him he could keep it.

Low Theory

Self-Portrait in a Mess of Lines

The ending is right behind us, watching
Confused, having to switch hands and accept
Decades later, a new and different sense
Of linearity. No one ever
Opens a book that way and begins with
Many pencils, tight, in a rubber band
Learning, again, how to write their own name
No pencil works alone. It's never just
Scarring at the wrist and lost sensation
Nodding along to the empty music
This elegy won't write itself. A bruise
Serene one day, having gotten used to
The speed and spread of blood, the color of
Remembering. Sometimes it is useful

O'Keeffe

It's not always useful to remember
Ripping the canvas. Paint flakes and begins
Trying to walk without a hitch. It's like
The beginning of devotion. I look
Hoping to retain the original
Pain, or the shape of it spreading
I sit and listen to the docent and
Rose light cools the nervous system, prevents
Further damage to the composition
It happened years ago but I can still
Orion, as if it broke the mesa
Beneath the skin. Never before had I
A long conversation with the body
It was never a minor jealousy

A Love Poem

As if there were a minor jealousy
Birds settling on a wire. Forgive me, the
Same as before the virus. I couldn't
I was at the airport, watching someone's
Sort of like that. If it's a palimpsest
To see rain clouds taxi through the blinds
We mean when we say of the children, they
Forced open the flower, or needed to
He said. Sometimes the language we borrow
The bell rings all the time but the bell is
Crows fighting in the trees. And suddenly
This is the one I was talking about
If we had more time—it's always like that
Years later, to keep the frames on the wall

The Gardner Heist

It’s been twenty years but they keep the frames
Beneath the wrist. It missed the artery
Storm on the Sea of Galilee and two
Or three days after surgery. They said
Now in the many millions, the reward
Would never come back. Not now, not ever
Looking online at the original
Refusing parallel movement, the hands
Those empty frames. Imagine holding a
Memory—or was it a photograph
Conservators in panic. Damage to
The median nerve, the hand gone suddenly
And for all these years without a suspect
Undoing all sensation, even pain

Meditation at Hunters Point

It is the work of feeling to undo
Batteries rolling under the backseat
Another year in the books. So attached
Tonally questionable, and I ask
Less and less until the radio is
Like pain, after it's ended. Just a shape
Brushed to this or that side of memory
So quickly I begin to doubt the whole
Reason for parking on a yellow curb
Sparrows, urgent from some near thicket
Of course, if *it* is the soul, and if *it*
Cannot remember the phrase, exactly
Same knot as yesterday, same pattern, the
Task is to forget. Forget it by heart

Concerto for the Left Hand

The task, of course, is to forget the whole
Body downward, lifting the head toward
Far bridges, cars streaming music. Lights too
Without meaning it. Breath the engine of
Less is more when it comes to temptation
Wandering, and alone, past so many
Inherited features. Early onset
Collision up ahead by the station
And pain, eventually. Walking slow or
Letting go those cemented trains of thought
A burning sensation. That's what the pills
In a different language, the same question
Never as fulfilling as the last time
The afternoon, and it begins to rain

Palimpsest

This afternoon the rain begins. You make
Every dog-eared corner torn at the fold
And pain touches the mind, familiar
Rush. The way grain opens into color
Is said to sponsor feeling, or was that
You in the mirror. You drinking coffee
A friend on the stoop, but the call button
Responds to water by curling. It needs
It exists. And so does pain, especially
Hue and tint, a blue wash to make it seem
Instead of pills. The body can only
With a ruler or pencil follow the
Rain needling the carpet. You go to close
The same book since college. It's just that good

Kouros

The same book since college. It's just that good
Frame 10 demonstrates how marble stays cool
Telling the truth without oversharing
My scar was showing, so I put my hand
Historically speaking, over the moon
Wounding the sculpture in transit. It's so
Surprised to touch it, to be allowed to
Watch the pigment flower in late day sun
Some pages stick and do not turn, or turn
Tons of it, pink, from a Tennessee mine
Imagining a conversation with
Limited sensation in the fingers
Awake, remembering all that starlight

Memento Mori

Awake, remembering all that starlight
Come morning when the mail arrives, or if
Drenched in summer rain. My brother, when he
Doesn't turn up in dreams anymore and
Props open the screen door with a package
Because, after all, not every star is
In the forecast. But the forecast never
Until he checked himself in. That phone call
Lived, as kids, next to a creek that would flood
And tear open the envelope. Without
Knowing how far away it is or if
By shaking you can tell what's in it. Just
Hearing her, the nurse, say it out loud
The sound of rain is the sound of breaking

Personal Weather

The sound of rain is the sound of breaking
Stages we all go through eventually
In recurring dreams, or so the book says
One who is looked at and the one who looks
At last into the gulf. Then it begins
Beginning to question the narrative
Ecosystem, nesting in near ponds
Family, too, these days. Blooming apart
And what does that say about organized
Quiet—a talisman when it's your turn
From very far or very close, making
As love might, toward it. The estuary
Surrounds herself with friends and loved ones, all
Ways of wondering, what would happen if

Stichomythia

I've been wondering what would happen if
From across the parking lot, an old friend
Dropped one by one into the teller's palm
More fog, less rain. This cough won't go away
Yelling, I know, won't turn red to green or
These feelings into the future. We're as sick as
The world, if we are still calling it that
Time enough to stop, shake hands, ask after
And before leaving the pharmacy I
Write about the weather to distract from
My grip, too weak to reciprocate his
Family and work. We have so little to
Do but sit and wait for the light to change
The way we experience a picture

Basquiat

The way we experience a picture
Tomorrow, wielding color immediate
But not before dinner. That jacket is
First in the family to move out, move on
The blue shadow of a house. But suppose
No particular school of painting or
To be alive now. We owe that to his
Process, every fiber, the attention
To spare. But just like that it's October
Silver when the light hits. Think of each coat
So ill he had to stay behind. No one
Fell or is falling but the leaves are still
The cheapest available, which matters
Crushes, dissolves the blue one at breakfast

What the Water Gave Me, 1938

I crush the blue one at breakfast, dissolve
Under the influence of Khalo and
Being O-negative. It saved my life
From self-portraiture to entire cities
Sitting for hours in the tub. Better to
Go hungry then be in pain or pretend
To look the viewer, always, in the eye
By noon, though I forgot to take that dose
So many reproductions it loses
Something feral in the background. A cat
A more compassionate Marxism
Without the dizziness, the side effects
I find a bench and try not to project
Touch. Or another person, answering

Domestic Timelapse

They answered as always, from the other
Staircase, wooden as it is, and aging
That life so churned in the silence I took
Over easy, poking the yolk with bread
Until the neighbors called. The music, they
Almost shut the door on my forefinger
Intentionally omitting the word
Splitting an avocado. We never
Despite their sudden outburst, carried on
Not unless I cried out of earshot or
Without burning the toast. So much of this
Room, though drowned out by the television
Relied on them for sustenance. In fact
Levity, a hard word for kids to say

Portrait of Edith Schiele, 1918

No coincidence that brevity rhymes
And relishes the curl at line's end. Not
Describing the hand, but where the hand meets
And becomes smudged. The body's implied
Composition, coupling longevity with
The index finger, smearing chalk—see how
His ability to stop, knowing when
Within a week they'll both have gone—artist
Formless or, within the unformed, a thought
Wandering the paper's low, far corner
The word soul, for example. The way she
Avoiding the right hand, must contemplate
To say blue would do no justice to the
Ending, which is right behind us, watching

Leaving the Party

I was a shopper in a dark aisle: stoplights, squares of gum-pocked cement, a camera store called Shuttered. I was walking at midnight down Granada Ave with no cell phone, knowing the time from the sign at the bank I'd passed three or four blocks ago. Or maybe it was a credit union. It may be obvious now, but the vacancies were a metaphor: store windows in the dark, raccoons—three or four of them—emerging from the condemned craftsman near Byrd Park and standing on their hind legs, unbothered by the rain. It was raining then. It'd begun to spit. Attention, a person named Jenny had said, is our last and most precious resource—she poured a mixed drink and handed it to me, unfamiliar with my history—types of, scales of, ways to give and receive. I needed water and fresh air. Do you ever feel your phone vibrate when you are without it? Twin chirps of a car horn at an empty intersection? Now and then I think about how certain stars are inaccessible to the gaze, directly, so you have to look at the adjacent stars, ingest them in the periphery. Yes, I took a sip. Maybe two. But once the gin bloomed I put down the red cup and excused myself. The porchlight flickered when I stepped out, then settled. Drinking isn't the problem, my brother said once—we were driving back late from Uncle Terry's service, six or seven ticks below the speed limit—the problem is *drinking*. He was like that; I always sort of knew what he meant. That night on Granada I had someone to call but nothing to call them with. The one car I saw go by had one of those Jesus fish on the back, but with a hook in its mouth, a sort of joke I guess. It slowed but did not stop at the red light. I don't know why I didn't go back for the phone. I'd have to return the next day, knock, ask for Jenny. The rain wasn't stopping or speeding up, and when I turned to pass the parking garage on University I could hear someone in there, high up practicing a wind instrument, maybe a flute. Two or three times before I'd heard this but it was usually a band practicing, a small group, percussive, imprecise. I pulled off and stood under the awning of the salon next door. Before he died my brother had gone on a real bender—eighteen or twenty beers a day, the nurse said. He'd been calling in sick at the lumber yard but still took shifts in the ambulance, night shifts in the North End. Maybe you know what this is like, hearing music overlayed with rain. They stop competing after a while: low thrum on acrylic canvas, continuous glissando, widening stream in the margin of the street.

San Francisco

Last day for the Rivera mural; we can see a narrow section from over the near rail. Against a ribbon of hills and low sky one man swings a hammer, another an axe.

It's Monday, and mostly we are alone. She doesn't ask about my brother, and I don't ask about the apartment above Café Leon. We'd shared a cigarette in the window there.

In a month, from London, she'll send a photo. Grass against a stone fence. Steam. Orange sky behind three-day clouds. The path will be hard mud and the photo will come with no caption.

We go between the two Richter galleries, abstract then figural, the rooms separated by a narrow wall. The docent slips into the hall, so we are alone on a bench, looking together at a piece called *Fenster*, German for "window."

Light from the city hits Judd's boxes; she checks the time on her phone. She calls me Danny. "To confer importance," is what Sontag said—to photograph is to confer importance.

She holds a table for us, a spot by the window. There is white graffiti on the adjacent building, though I cannot make out what it says.

She drinks the last of my tea and we sit a while. Again the Rivera, a group of middle schoolers on a tour. I part a curtain of gold beads to ask the docent for a water fountain, and she tells me I've entered through the exit of an installation.

For three years

after my brother died I was a painter. After work I'd park my truck and roll a hashworm in tobacco, then address the easel on the kitchen counter. Acrylic was cheapest, and I let it cake on the faux-marble. I had studied architecture, but never painting, so I didn't know how to render faces or hands, couldn't mix the colors I wanted to see. At some point in the evening I'd make a gin and tonic.

I learned sometime later the word "underpainting"—what is painted, then painted over, covered entirely with subsequent layers of paint. Textures and shapes survive, though the viewer perceives only the outermost contours, seams or faint ripples across the surface. I'd sometimes have friends over and ask them to make marks or write phrases, flick water on the dry acrylic.

I would stream *The Köln Concert* from my phone, tell D and J to do something interesting. We'd been in a ketamine phase and I watched them from the couch, their slow bodies in yellow stove light. Then I only heard them, and from far away.

My brother was not a painter; he was an EMT, a drinker, then a photo on the counter. He never met these particular friends, whose names push out from beneath one of my better paintings. He drove the same Toyota sedan as D, though, who drove most nights, and never woke me before he left.

Puddle Jumper

I don't know who on this plane is grieving and who's playing pool on their phone. Who's really sleeping and who's closed their eyes for some time apart. During takeoff I raised the window shade and when the pilot banked left I could make out downtown Los Angeles breaching a sea of bright intersections, dark contours, simple void where Santa Monica and Venice and Malibu meet the ocean. Necklace of lights. Black velvet. To call a name out over water is, in the novel open on my knee now, a ceremony of forgetting, the name taken without echo into the boundless Pacific churn. I turn to mention this to Gabby but her eyes are closed, her earbuds in. The plane slips into a cloud. I doubt it, the man in the seat in front of me says—his wife had asked if he thought the kids were behaving for someone named Jodi, if he thought they'd gone down for the evening. Everything, even on these short flights, sponsors feeling. Reading lights down the aisle, flicking on or off. A stranger's cough muffled or held in. I bet Kevin's fine actually, he says, but you know how Maya is when we're away. I let the air from an overhead vent lift the edge of a page, then another; I lose my place. When we were younger my brother spoke of a particular desolation he experienced at eating too many olives. He'd spoon them from the jar listening to music or watching *Spirited Away* on his laptop. Since Gabby moved in I've been talking about him more, mining our years together, composing the brother-in-law she might've had, eventually. The sea. The mountains. Central Valley seen from a nighttime cloud. It's all the same now, dark and diminishing as I lower the window shade. I take a bag of pretzels when they come around, leave it on the tray table for Gabby. She used to eat the olives from her dad's martinis. Salt is kind of at the center of the novel, the shallow salt flats south of Pichilemu. I've not gotten to the part where he tries to leave, but I know he drowns. So many references to breath, to sound and its absence. Endless, he says about the Pacific at night, hard and endless. A voice over the PA: initial descent. Gabby takes out an earbud but keeps her eyes closed; she says, Hi sweetie. And I say, Hi sweetie, and press her tray table into its little lock and set the pretzels in her lap. And the man in front of me says he'll call when they land. And the cabin tips forward, and little by little the pressure drops. It's okay, his wife says, let them sleep. My brother liked sitting alone on planes; he liked having space. I'd look around for his headphones during landing—the bulky ones that cover your ears—I'd look around so I could find him getting off the plane. Now the cabin illuminates. They do a final pass with the garbage bag. Gabby's back asleep and I know I should wake her. I should wake her now, before we touch down in Oakland.

On Photography

I’ve quit smoking and am dreaming again, have been needing
to run my hand over the quilt,
                              name three smells, three things I see nearby.
I crack the window.
                              Rain in the city is a dirty smell, and I see
the flesh of my arm unlit in the steel window frame.

Before G left for Spokane we brought the Polaroid
into the bedroom and said what we feared in each other.
I liked
what her shoulders did with the word *casual*.

                                        She took the camera and told me
not to lie. She likened the photographer to a Zen archer
                                                                      —something
about having, first, to become the target. She didn’t have
to tell me to look when she pressed the shutter.
                                        I light a match and let it burn
on the counter—little scar on the tile.
                                                      In the dream tonight
I was with David in his mother’s closet, putting my hands
up the sleeves of a dark fur coat.
          He smelled like grass, and we’d lost track of time.

Notebook Fragments

It's April and all my friends are married. The Japanese maples, in their pots on the balcony, need to be weeded and pruned.

The reds and yellows of autumn leaves are there all the time, I read. But we only see them in dead or dying leaves, in the absence of chlorophyll.

The cruelest month—who said that?

Reading the posthumous Ashbery—five unfinished longer works—I pay more attention to his xeroxed drafts than to the finished poems. *Edge* becomes *hedge*. *Rigorous*, *peaceful*. At the bottom of each typescript page, a date and location.

For to be finished
is nothing. Only children and dinosaurs like endings

On my desk: beeswax candle, lit / three twisted stacks of books / loose: Joanna Walsh's *My Life As a Godard Movie* / two gold hoops / tiger balm / G's water bottle, with her company slogan, *Come see what we see*, on the side.

Ashbery loved film. He watched Turner Classic Movies in his basement in Hudson, talking to friends on the phone.

My therapist suggests I journal in present tense; she says it might encourage epiphany.

I open the windows for a cross breeze; reminds me of summer in Kentucky, waiting in bed for the room to cool.

"It's after ten on a November morning nine years ago"—a sentence written in the present about the past—"light through narrow leaves makes an easy pattern on the sidewalk."

G gets back tonight—a work retreat in Portland. I've left her chicken sausage and rice on the stove.

She climbs onto me in bed, asks if I'll tell her what I told my therapist this week.

All language left in the air, without a response, starts to sound crazy, or like poetry.

Skillings includes, on page 115, a handwritten draft of "An Unspecified Amount." The handwriting is legible but not neat.

Ashbery's lines, though, sit atop each other like skinny books or sheets of paper.

I can't tell through the window what's late traffic on MacArthur and what is wind in the trees.

Epiphany: night jasmine smells the way candy necklaces taste

Later, G long asleep: midnight across the floor, dim and blue.

In a dream, I wake with her in a cottage on the leeward side of Eleuthera. Peter and Olivia are gone, already in the water, the sun blood orange through the horizon.

You're allowed to ask questions, my therapist says, you just might not get answers.

The difference between adults and children is the ability to pause between stimulus and response. G says so.
"I bring this up not as an accusation, but as a means of deepening with you."

Regarding his practice, Ashbery spoke of a current or stream he drew from, little by little, every day. "I don't look on poems as closed works," he wrote, "I feel they're probably going on all the time . . . and I occasionally snip off a length."

G's attic: rack of light jackets / eucalyptus sprig on the windowsill / mattress on the floor / low altar with candle / yoga mat, purple and made of cork

The winds that lie
in the mind,
the ruinous winds

In her garden, Louise says my work suffers under the speaker, that I should consider removing the *I*.

Ashbery would argue sometimes with translators. You can't say that in French, they would explain, referencing an out-of-place noun, verbs in clashing tenses. And Ashbery would reply, you can't say it in English either.

G says to keep her out of poems for a while, *unless it feels, actually, like a love poem.*

Addicted to processing?

Have been trying instead to include my cat in as many poems as possible. Louise says either he's a red herring or, once in a while, the emotional center of the piece.

I wonder at the terms "linguistic malleability" and "tonal virtuosity" which, according to Skillings, made it difficult for Ashbery to remember which language—English or French—was his.

Overshared to Jalen about our sex life. G punches me in the shoulder when I tell her, southbound on the 5 near Mendota.

Why do we out ourselves?

"The true content of a photograph is invisible, for it derives from a play not with form, but with time."

Epiphany: no one lets anyone else scroll their photo library

Dream of a potted orange tree small enough to live on top of desk. Oranges the size of marbles, blossoms unfisting white among waxy leaves.

At the farmers market a man named Earl Ochre sells Topanga honey, touches G on the arm. The Ochres go back 100 years in Los Angeles, he says, since the valley was just avocado groves and citrus.

Every year at this time of day I get a feeling
of a pain, like roses and dried figs.

Overheard by the kraut stand: the four bodily humors—phlegm, yellow bile, blood, and melancholy

Poppies everywhere in Adams Point. Silk teacups in the yard, citrus orange. Little spills across the median on MacArthur.

I call them feminine; G calls me basic.

As on a festal day in early spring
The tidelands maneuver and the air is quick with imitations

Sitting with the phrase "genius for deferral," which I've found in my notes, unattributed.

I scratch the cat's neck while G smokes on the balcony, next to the maples. The red one is sturdy and full, vertical in its reach. The green splits, somehow, into two little trees, bent in their directions.

Likeness

I saw this guy tonight in Adams Point, by the lake—the sun was getting low, so I'd taken a break from grading—this guy in one of the green Carhartt jackets smoking by the water. The light was really orange and in his face, and when he turned my way for a second, I don't know, I just needed to check in on you. Is the ginger coming in okay, or did you have to dig it out? I was telling Gabby about your backyard; it's really something. Two or three times this year I walked through the botanical garden and thought to send you a photo of the bunny orchid; it's purple and white and blue and flowers best in June, near the solstice. Sorry to hear about Luna; she was a really sweet cat. One of the last times I hung out with Matty we packed lips in his apartment and talked a lot about Dad. I know your relationship was a little different, so I don't wanna make things weird, but he told me how Dad slapped him around this one time as a kid. Matty's paintball gun discharged in the house and broke a pane of glass. I guess Dad took him out to eat, after, that steakhouse off Palumbo, and let him drink a beer with his burger. He was telling me this and spitting into an empty Dasani bottle. His jacket wasn't green and it wasn't a Carhartt but it was that same style, impenetrable knit with the hood. I just stood there by the lake looking at the guy for a second too long probably, and he kind of got weirded out. He mean-mugged and shrugged at me. The fuck are you looking at? I turned home early, and I had to take the long way since the gardens close at sundown. I'm back home now, watching the sky above the city get all purple and dark, a little white where the stars come in. Now that Gabby's moved in I'm never really alone, but she's out tonight, drinking mezcal on Grand with a friend. The last thing he said before I left his apartment—he'd screwed the blue cap on his Dasani bottle and walked me to the door—was that I should get my brake lines checked. I guess he'd heard something when I pulled in. Now whenever I hear that whining sound when a car pulls up to the stop sign by our building, I think of him and that dingy apartment. I remember how big he seemed inside that jacket when I clapped him once on the shoulder and stepped out through the open screen door. He was holding it for me.

Calder in Motion

I am one of two on the 19th Street platform. South Oakland freight containers, matte in morning light, are stacked in neat grids by the water. Not the ocean, but the flat harbor. The other man wears a gold hoop and checks his phone, and when the ten-door to Millbrae arrives, he does not look up.

As a rule, I do not enter museums on an empty stomach. The single notecard I'm allowed in the exhibition is stained now, on one side, with avocado. And each time the train stops, the bright glass towers have swollen a little into focus.

The artist once traded a mobile for a shed in the south of France. The shed became his workspace. He installed tall windows, and on a clear day, through a narrow opening in the pines, he could see the Mediterranean.

There's a man at the top of the stairs in the atrium, solo saxophone on the loudspeakers. He points his disposable camera at a couple ascending, shoulders rubbing. The last time I was here, there was no music.

It is a Q-tip the size of an arm, what the curator calls "her Calder push stick." The mobiles are designed to hang outdoors and for a high degree of variability of motion—whether by wind or human force, no two movements will be the same. She strikes one of the red spades like a gong.

It was a visit to Mondrian's studio that inspired the bold reds and yellows, the industrial wire. The room is warm and near capacity. The terrace is open. Through the glass—from a strip of city sun—a child watches, points, then motions for his father to put him down.

To the Wedding

In the morning she reads

while I cut papaya
the way her mother taught me—

no fruit left on the skin.

She reads and I try to write a novel
that is stolen, mostly, from our life—

her job, my fear
of other men, our Thai spot on Piedmont.

She's skeptical of the endeavor.

Berger's signalman spends most of that novel in transit.

The headlight of his motorbike dims in fog,
the early alpine dark.

He leaves Valenza, and on a straightaway
along the south bank of the Po

he pulls over to pray.

Gabby and I share a membership at Costco.

From the parking lot
we can see across the bay

to San Francisco.

She makes a grid of paper towels
in the pantry.

I slip the little tag back
into the neck of her shirt.

The signalman does make it, eventually—
in time to eat lucioperca and dance

and watch Gino undo one of his daughter's braids.

The story ends
the way most do.

Not with the band packing up
nor with glasses emptied into the chill grass—

she dies slowly; Gino watches,
puts droplets of water into her dry mouth.

"No you don't," Gabby says sometimes
when I tell her I love her,

"You don't know anything about love—"

I put the papaya on the table
in a bowl

in cubes as neat as I can manage.

She tents the book on her knee.

Thirty-three

Could be half my life, could be all of it. Could be a third, Gabby said, raising a glass of a chilled orange wine the server described as funky. Evenings in Berkeley condescended to words like funky, the wealthy down from the hills for a plate of gnocchi and delicata squash, shimmering headlights across the rain-streaked window. I had little interest in ninety-nine, but didn't say so. Over and again that week we'd talked about time—types of, ways to measure and experience, the colonial origins of time systems—and one night became unspeakably aroused at the distinction between time as a universal fact and time as contained by a round plastic clock with tick marks and numbers and sharp-pointed arms. At some point our neighbor Gloria banged on the wall, and the next day we had to buy her flowers, write a little note. My brother died when he was twenty-eight, I said to Gabby, I'm five years older now than my older brother—it wasn't sympathy I was looking for but language—It's OK, I'm OK, just having an experience. The server came with a tiny wicker basket of bread. Gabby had read a book about time, and learned there exist certain apps that determine how many years we each have left to live. Check the box next to the foods you eat three or more times a week. On average, how many miles do you walk each day? Do you live alone? We did it there at the table, leaning back when the server came with our salads. Tomato and burrata. Arugula, lemon juice, parm. She waited for me to finish so we could click the submit button at the same time, but when we did a little screen came up prompting us to upgrade to premium—$5.99/month to see your remaining time on earth, chart your progress as you make meaningful changes to your lifestyle. Long before he died I had this fleeting sense, now and then, that I would outlive my brother. For sure he didn't live well—the WoFo Reserve, the hot browns—but even when we were kids he had this way of saying things. He refused a pocket watch from our grandfather, for instance, said he couldn't bear taking from his grandfather something with such sentimental value—I guess our great-grandfather had brought it from Wrocław. A man who dies at twenty-eight was, his whole life, a man who was going to die at twenty-eight. Our grandpa gave it to me a few years later, for my birthday. Or there was that stretch in middle school when the *illmatic* album resonated with him in a way I didn't really understand, especially the song and chorus everyone knows—I'd hear it through his closed door on loop some nights, and I would sometimes repeat the lyrics myself at school to friends. These moments and experiences all started to overlay one another at the restaurant. I was hugging my grandfather on University Ave in Berkeley, thanking him for the watch. I was eating hot browns with Gabby outside my brother's door. Really, the salad was delicious and I said so, and I took Gabby's hand; she'd finished her wine and the couple next to us had gone. I told her how crazy it is—this time last year we didn't even know each other. I said the watch works great, just needs a little winding. I forgive you for drinking and dying and that thing you said in Orlando about my teeth. Happy birthday, Gabby said, netting her fingers into mine. Tuna carpaccio. Boar ragù with new potatoes and broccolini. An even pour of the orange wine.

The Fayette County Line

I drive out Old Frankfort Pike past the ditch
by the creek where you pulled off on New Year's Day
to pick from the mud that Jack Russell
with swollen nipples and bring her back to the farm.

You called her Jillie Bean.

It's fall here, the window cracked, and a box on the floor
in back holds my share of your ashes.

A slash ahead in the pasture: some other creek
must've flooded overnight. It's overtaken the road
to Windy Corner—you loved the house sauce
        at the market there
and the hash browns, the way Ouita, when you came in,
called you *kiddo.*

I was away at school
but you said the dog, that first night, left
these little stains on your clothes at the foot of the bed
but didn't whimper or cry.

You shortened her name to Jillie, then Bean—bizarre
that she outlived you.

Dad had to bring her in last year.

I slow and stop your Volvo in the road
a few feet short of the water
and roll down the window.

I put my hand through to gauge the wind.

Notes

The epigraph comes from John Berger's *Ways of Seeing*.

The "book on my desk" referenced in "The Clarinet" is *Cubism/Futurism* by Max Kozloff.

A note on "Low Theory": A crown of sonnets is a series of fifteen consecutive sonnets linked, usually, by their first and last lines. The last line of sonnet one becomes the first line of sonnet two; the last line of sonnet two becomes the first line of sonnet three. The series continues this way until the final line of the entire series, which is a repetition of the first line of the first sonnet.

In composing "Low Theory," I used this structure as a container for a sort of meditation, through poetry, on the ideas and experiences presented in the essay that precedes it. The injury to my hand. Cubist representation. Non-binary knowledge practices. The crown draws procedural inspiration from Lerner's *Mean Free Path*. By this I mean there is no single way through these sonnets; I personally experience them much the way I experience Braque, encountering with each read associations and potential meanings I had previously skipped over or forgotten, or sometimes had not even intended. For those who choose to read it, I wish you many experiences. I hope your gaze lands where it lands, that for you the rain never reaches ground.

The notion of the photographer as a Zen archer in my poem "On Photography" is borrowed from Susan Sontag, from her seminal work *On Photography.*

"Notebook Fragments": As the title suggests, this poem is composed of text I transcribed from several of the notebooks I used from 2022–2024. I've done my best, here, to provide proper attribution for language borrowed from other writers. Please excuse any discrepancies; my notebooks are very messy.

The note about autumn leaves and chlorophyll is borrowed and modified from Ben Lerner's short story "The Ferry," as is "All language left in the air, without a response, starts to sound crazy, or like poetry."

The posthumous Ashbery I reference is *Parallel Movement of the Hands*, edited by Emily Skillings, with a foreword by Ben Lerner. The lines I've cited in italics throughout "Notebook Fragments" all come from this collection.

The phrase "the cruelest month" is T. S. Eliot's, from *The Waste Land.*

The quotation "The true content of a photograph is invisible, for it derives from a play, not with form, but with time" comes from John Berger's *Understanding a Photograph.*

The four bodily humors I cite (phlegm, yellow bile, blood, and melancholy) come from Valeria Luiselli's *Sidewalks*, as does the sentence "It's after ten on a November morning nine years ago."

•

This book engages with a number of artists, exhibits, and individual art pieces. I've compiled, below, as comprehensive a list as I could manage of these artists and works, in order of their appearance in the book:

Alexander Calder: Dissonant Harmony, SFMOMA, July 3, 2021—Ongoing.

Gerhard Richter, *Lesende* (1994), oil on linen; and *Tisch* (1962), oil on canvas

Anish Kapoor, *Vortex* (2004); fiberglass, lacquer, wood

Julie Mehretu, *HOWL, eon (I, II)* (2017), ink and acrylic on canvas

Georges Braque, *The Clarinet* (1913), papier collé; and *Still Life: Violin and Candlestick* (1910), oil on canvas

Man Ray *Untitled* (1922), gelatin silver print

The Georgia O'Keeffe Museum, Santa Fe, New Mexico

The Isabella Stewart Gardner Museum, Boston, Massachusetts

Frida Kahlo *What the Water Gave Me* (1938), oil on canvas

Egon Schiele, *Portrait of Edith Schiele* (1918), lead and watercolor on paper

Pablo Picasso, *Still Life with Mandolin* (1924), oil on canvas

Georgia O'Keeffe, *Horse's Skull with Pink Rose* (1931), oil on canvas

René Magritte, *The Treachery of Images* (1929), oil on canvas

Mark Rothko, *White Center* (1957), oil on canvas

Diego Rivera's America, SFMOMA, July 16, 2022—January 3, 2023

Gerhard Richter, *Fenster* (2002), oil on linen

Donald Judd, *To Susan Buckwalte*r (1964); galvanized iron, aluminum, and lacquer

Acknowledgments

Many thanks to the editors of the following publications, where poems from this manuscript first appeared, some in different form:

American Poetry Review: "Notebook Fragments"
The Atlantic: "Likeness"
Boston Review: "Leaving the Party"
Literary Hub: "Low Poetics: A Meditation"
Los Angeles Review of Books: "A Love Poem"
The New Yorker: "Thirty-three"
Poetry Society of America: "Calder"
Virginia Quarterly Review: "Man Ray," "San Francisco," "The Fayette County Line," "The Lake," "*Tisch*"
ZYZZYVA: "The Köln Concert"

"Calder" received the Lucille Medwick Memorial Award from *Poetry Society of America*, selected by Jennifer Elise Foerster.

Thanks to the folks at Liveright/W. W. Norton, especially my brilliant editor, Gina Iaquinta.

Thank you to the following institutions for their support: the Creative Writing departments at San Diego State University and

Stanford University, the Kenyon Review Summer Writing Workshops, and the San Francisco Museum of Modern Art (SFMOMA).

For their time, attention, and care, thank you Sandra Alcosser, David Baker, Victoria Chang, aracelis girmay, Louise Glück, Richie Hofmann, Amaud Jamaul Johnson, A. Van Jordan, Patrick Phillips, and Richard Siken. And special thanks to Blas Falconer—a true mentor and friend.

These poems, on their way to becoming a book, were graced by a lot of brilliant poets and thinkers. Thanks in particular to Austin Araujo, Brent Ameneyro, Jade Cho, Brian Cochran, Jackson Holbert, Joseph Rios, Cintia Santana, Ajibola Tolase, Alison Thumel, and Dāshaun Washington.

Jalen Eutsey and Christell Victoria Roach, thank you for your friendship and belief, and for those nights loitering in various Oakland restaurants past closing.

Love and thanks to Harrison Hoffman and Peter Cable.

Mom, Dad, and Caleigh—thank you for your love, patience, and unwavering support. And to my brother, Matty, the real writer in the family: I miss you every day.

And Gabby. No poem or book or accumulation of books could render what it is to wake and move through these days with you, this life we've made. But I'll keep trying. I love you.